Lebanon's Hezbollah

Ann Byers

The Rosen Publishing Group, Inc.
New York

To my husband, Steve,
my indispensable partner in research and in life

Published in 2003 by The Rosen Publishing Group, Inc.
29 East 21st Street, New York, NY 10010

Copyright © 2003 by The Rosen Publishing Group, Inc.

First Edition

Library of Congress Cataloging-in-Publication Data

Byers, Ann.
Lebanon's Hezbollah / by Ann Byers.— 1st ed.
    v. cm. — (Inside the world's most infamous terrorist organizations)
Summary: Recounts the historical origins, philosophy, and most notorious attacks of the Hezbollah terrorist group, including information on their present activities, possible future course of action, and counter-terrorism efforts directed against them.
Includes bibliographical references and index.
Contents: A region in turmoil—Resistance movement or terrorist group?—Hezbollah vs. the United States—Evolution of a terrorist organization.
ISBN 0-8239-3821-2
1. Hizballah (Lebanon) 2. National liberation movements—Lebanon.
[1. Hizballah (Lebanon) 2. Terrorism—Lebanon.]
I. Title. II. Series.
JQ1828.A98 H6234 2002
303.6'25'095692—dc21
                                                        2002010602

Manufactured in the United States of America

Contents

Introduction

From the air, Shebaa Farms looks like a picture postcard. Shadowed by the snow-capped peaks of majestic Mount Hermon, this strip of land that separates Israel from Lebanon is beautiful. It is a narrow band of green hills, dry riverbeds, and cool mountain springs. Small villages with blue-roofed houses dot the countryside, and goats graze in open pastures. From the air, the scene is lovely.

From the ground, however, the idyllic picture disintegrates. The green hills are spotted with scorched black patches where rockets have blasted and burned the pastureland. The roads between villages are rutted with holes where bombs have blown away asphalt as well as cars and trucks. Many of the white-washed homes have broken windows, shattered walls, and yards littered with the remnants of exploded mortar shells. Some villages are completely deserted.

Tanks, military trucks, and armored cars patrol the streets. Helicopters circle overhead, and armies practice their drills with live ammunition. Lebanese people on their way to work are killed by roadside bombs intended for Israeli soldiers. Families hanging their wash on the line take cover when they hear the popping of machine guns or the whistle of mortar rounds. Children at play are crippled when hidden land mines detonate.

Tripoli is the second largest city in Lebanon and an important port. It is also a commercial and industrial center, as well as a popular beach resort for northern Lebanon. Though a productive and scenic city, Tripoli has seen its share of violence throughout its history. Originally founded by the Phoenicians, the city suffered wave after wave of invasions by Persians, Muslim Arabs, Christian Crusaders, Egyptians, Ottomans, and the French. In 1958 and 1975 the city was the center of revolts against the Christian Lebanese government. In 1985 Syria took control of Tripoli and still maintains it today.

Throughout this tiny, bloody patch of land, two different flags fly. The blue and white banner of Israel had flown over parts of Lebanon since 1978, when Israel first invaded its neighbor to stop and prevent attacks upon its own territory launched from the region. Its possession of the Shebaa Farms, however, dates even earlier.

A schoolchild crosses a United Nations checkpoint in the Lebanese village of Zibquine on February 2, 2000, soon after Israeli warplanes raided the area. Zibquine lies just north of the south Lebanon occupation zone Israel maintained until its withdrawal from southern Lebanon in May 2000.

Introduction

Israel first captured the Shebaa Farms area in 1967, during the Six-Day War with Egypt, Syria, and Jordan. It considers the Shebaa Farms territory to have belonged to Syria before then. Therefore, Israel claims it is not occupying Lebanese territory. Instead, it claims to lawfully occupy land won during wartime. Syria, in turn, claims to have officially given the Shebaa Farms to Lebanon in 1951.

And during all that time, a small band of Lebanese warriors has fought fiercely to tear down this symbol of Israel and replace it with its own banner—a yellow flag stamped with a rifle and the words "Islamic Revolution of Lebanon." The group calls itself Hezbollah—the Party of God—a terrorist organization that is independent of the government of Lebanon.

Hezbollah, whose primary goals are the creation of an Islamic government in Lebanon and the destruction of the Jewish nation, has made expelling Israel from the area its mission. Its chief weapon is one it has used for more than twenty years with deadly consequences: terror. Though in 2000 Israel withdrew from every area of Lebanon except the Shebaa Farms, Hezbollah wants every last trace of the Israeli occupation removed from Lebanon—the foreign governments that support Israel, the United Nations troops that try to keep the peace, the Lebanese who cooperated with Israel during the occupation, and the Israeli soldiers still occupying a small part of Lebanese territory. For Hezbollah, however, the ouster from Lebanon of everything remotely related to the Israeli presence is only the beginning.

A Region in Turmoil

Hezbollah's grievances are not simply about land or even the Israeli occupation. They are not just about events of the last twenty or thirty years. The struggle in Lebanon is part of the larger conflict simmering throughout the entire Middle East and dating from ancient times.

A Nation Exiled

From about 1050 BC to 586 BC—a period of less than 500 years—the kingdom of Judea and Israel occupied a sliver of land on the eastern shore of the Mediterranean Sea, land the Israelites believed was promised to them by God to their ancestor Abraham. Abraham was the head of a large family. The twelve descendents of Abraham's grandson Jacob formed the twelve tribes of Israel, and eventually these nomadic tribes were led to the so-called Promised Land by Moses, a man who had led the Israelites out of slavery in Egypt. The nation enjoyed stability within its new territory for only a brief period, historically speaking. When the nation of Babylon overpowered the kingdom in 586 BC, the Israelites were scattered among their neighbors. For hundreds of years, these exiles continued to dream of a return to the Promised Land.

That dream was especially strong in the late 1800s. All across Europe, waves of anti-Semitism—prejudice against Jews—threatened the homes and lives of many Jews. Persecuted

Jews looked to the land of the ancient kingdom as a place of safety. In 1886, Theodor Herzl published a book, *The Jewish State* (in the original German, *Juden Stat*), suggesting that the only way Jews could ever guarantee their own safety would be to form their own state. And, of course, that country should be situated in the Middle East, at the exact site of historic Israel as described in the Jewish Bible. This push for a Jewish state became known as Zionism. The name was taken from Mount Zion, the place where Jerusalem, the capital of the ancient kingdom, had been located.

Jews Settle in Palestine

The Zionist movement grew rapidly among Jews everywhere. Jews fleeing persecution in Russia and other countries began moving to what was once Israel and building homes there. By 1914, nearly 85,000 Jews lived in the land they believed belonged to them by divine right.

At that time, however, the land was not governed by the Jews, nor were they its only occupants. It was inhabited by a number of different Arab groups—peoples originally from the Arabian Peninsula who had moved north and settled throughout the region. It had been ruled by a series of different conquering nations. In 1917 to 1918, as World War I was winding to a close, the British— with the help of the Arabs—captured the area from the Ottoman Empire (which in 1922 became Turkey). England named the tract of land Palestine, a name for the area used by the Roman Empire in the first century AD and referring to the Philistines, one of the earliest groups to live there. So as Jews began moving into Palestine, it was occupied by Arabs and claimed by Great Britain.

The Arabs were not happy with either the Jewish settlements cropping up within and outside their cities or the continuing British occupation. They had expected the British to leave Palestine when the war ended. They wanted to finally establish their own country in this land they had lived on for hundreds of years under the rule of others. Jewish settlements and the increasing momentum behind Zionism threatened that hope. The Palestinian Arabs were afraid that they would not only lose this chance for independence but would also end up being ruled by these Jewish refugees from other nations. As a result, the Palestinians rioted, revolted, and attacked the Jewish settlements several times.

Despite the violence, mistrust, and ill will, the Jews continued to settle in Palestine. They came slowly at first, but when Nazi persecution drove Jews out of Germany and other European countries, they took refuge in Palestine in ever greater numbers. In 1935 alone, nearly 62,000 Jews immigrated to Palestine. The horrible suffering of the Jews during the Nazi Holocaust that was revealed in the days following the end of World War II in 1945 made people all over the world sympathetic to their cause. Many nations began to officially embrace Zionism, arguing that the only way to prevent another Holocaust against the Jews was to allow them to build a strongly defended nation of their own. As a result, many of Europe's postwar Jewish refugees were relocated to Palestine. Soon after the end of World War II, 608,000 Jews lived among 1,269,000 Palestinians.

The land was still governed by Britain, however, and it still had twice as many Arabs living on it as Jews. The British leaders were having difficulty formulating a solution that was fair to both sides. Both Arabs and Jews wanted the same land. Both thought they had a right to it. And neither wanted to share it with the other. Britain had made conflicting promises to both the Arabs and the Jews. Finally, the British turned the problem over to the United Nations (UN) to solve.

Israel Becomes a Nation

The UN (a multinational organization devoted to peaceful resolution of political conflict) created a plan in 1947 to partition, or divide, Palestine fairly evenly into a Jewish state and an Arab state. The lines were drawn so that most, but not all, of the Jewish settlements fell within the borders of the Jewish state proposed by the Zionists. Most, but not all, of the Arabs currently lived within what would become the Arab state. The West Bank of the Jordan River and the Gaza Strip along the Mediterranean Sea were to be included within the Arab state. The cities of Jerusalem and Bethlehem—which contain sites sacred to Jews, Muslims, and Christians alike—would be considered international zones, and neither country's exclusive territory.

The Jews accepted the proposal. It would give them their own country where a portion of their ancestral kingdom had been, even if the new nation would not include all the land they wanted. The Arabs rejected the plan, however. They had lived in the area for hundreds of years, they considered the Jews intruders, and they felt that all of Palestine belonged to them.

Due to this resistance, the UN plan never became a reality. As soon as the partition plan was announced, Palestinian Arabs rose up in anger against the Jewish settlements. Violence erupted throughout Palestine wherever Jews lived. The British, tired of trying to keep peace in the region, withdrew from the territory on

May 15, 1948. The same day, the Jewish leadership, following the provisions of the rejected UN plan, declared "the establishment of the Jewish State in Palestine, to be called the State of Israel."

Immediately, the armies of five Arab countries joined the Palestinian Arabs in protest. Before Israel was even a day old, forces from Egypt, Syria, Jordan, Iraq, and Lebanon invaded the new country, trying to reclaim its land for the Palestinian Arabs. The Arab armies were not used to working together in a coordinated way, however. They were outnumbered, outgunned, and outperformed by the Israeli Defense Force (IDF). In 1949, the UN arranged armistices (truces) between these Arab countries and their new neighbor, Israel.

In this war of independence, Israel won 2,000 square miles of territory in addition to what it would have had under the original UN plan. Under the peace agreements, Israel gave some of it back. Jordan received part of the West Bank, while Egypt took the Gaza Strip. There was no land left for an independent Palestinian state.

Palestinian Refugees

With the possibility of a Palestinian state evaporating and violence increasing in the region, more than 700,000 Palestinian Arabs fled the land now called Israel. They sought shelter in several countries, including Egypt, Lebanon, and Syria. With the exception of Jordan, these countries refused to allow them to become full citizens. Instead, they lived in crowded refugee camps, became stuck in poverty, and enjoyed few rights. They were people without homes and without a country. These increasingly angry and bitter Palestinian refugees had one desire: to destroy Israel and repossess their homeland.

As refugees, however, they had almost no power to achieve that aim. They were poor, scattered, and disorganized. They had no army

According to the United Nations Relief Works Agency (UNRWA), there are over 375,000 Palestinian refugees in Lebanon, 210,000 of whom live in refugee camps. Palestinian refugees face extreme hardships and poverty in Lebanon and are denied basic civil rights and the opportunity to work in seventy-two professions. UNRWA is the international organization given the primary responsibility of providing for the basic health, education, and social welfare of Palestinian refugees throughout Lebanon, Jordan, Syria, the West Bank, and the Gaza Strip.

and few weapons. Lacking the resources to form a regular army, the Palestinians resorted to "irregular" guerrilla tactics, such as bombing, sabotage, and kidnapping. They sneaked out of refugee camps, crept across the border, and attacked Israeli soldiers with stones and homemade bombs. They sabotaged Israeli businesses. They terrorized Israeli cities and civilian populations. And Israel fought back. When a refugee group in Jordan or Syria invaded an Israeli village, Israel sent in its soldiers or its planes against the attackers' refugee camps. When Palestinians in Lebanon raided the northern part of Israel, the IDF retaliated harshly against camps in Lebanon.

Most of the Arab countries surrounding Israel cheered the actions of the Palestinian guerrillas. These countries were Islamic nations, and they sympathized with the Palestinians, who shared their Muslim faith. They resented the intrusion of a non-Islamic state in a region they claimed as their own and refused to recognize Israel as a legitimate country. Together, they fought wars against Israel in 1956, 1967, and 1973. All of Israel's neighbors sided with the Palestinians. All except Lebanon.

Turmoil in Lebanon

Lebanon is unique in the Middle East. It is the only Arab nation with a large, strong, non-Muslim population. Most of the non-Muslims are Maronite Catholics—practicing a branch of Christianity founded by John Maron, a Lebanese monk of the seventh century AD—who live in the north. (Some traditions trace the church to a different John Maron, a monk of the fourth century.) Several different Muslim groups live in the south. The Maronites, who at first outnumbered the Muslims, controlled the government. The Maronite ruling party did not want to fight against Israel, so Lebanon did not take part in the Arab-Israeli wars that engulfed the rest of the region throughout the decades following the creation of Israel. Some of those wars enlarged Israel's territory, however, sending even more Palestinian refugees fleeing to Lebanon. By 1970, over 200,000 Palestinians lived in refugee camps in southern Lebanon.

The large number of Palestinian refugees changed the balance of power in Lebanon. Most of the refugees were Muslim, and they joined with Lebanese Muslims to try to take control of the country away from the Maronites. In 1975, a civil war erupted between the Maronite government and Islamic rebels. Israel, not wanting to lose its only friend in the region, supplied the Lebanese Christian forces with money and weapons.

Syria, an Islamic country, also entered the war on the side of the Lebanese Christian government, although for a different reason. It was afraid that Israel might try to take over Lebanon if the government began to lose to the Islamic rebels. When the civil war ended in 1976, the Maronites were still in control of the government, but Syria, with its 35,000 troops in Lebanon, had gained the real power. Relying on Syria's military muscle to preserve their government, the Maronites were forced to allow Syria to call most of the shots from then on. Many now consider Syria little more than an occupying force in Lebanon, controlling the outcome of elections and creating a parliament that will bend to its will. One of Syria's first decisions following the end of the civil war was to leave southern Lebanon, with its hundreds of thousands of Palestinian and non-Palestinian Muslims, to itself.

Without the approval of Syria, southern Lebanon became a haven for groups seeking to destroy Israel. In 1970, the Palestine Liberation Organization (PLO), a group of about 15,000 refugees

Who's Who in Hezbollah

Ali Atwa: One of the terrorists on TWA Flight 847, hijacked on June 14, 1985, while en route from Athens, Greece, to Rome, Italy; currently on the FBI's Most Wanted Terrorist list.

Sheikh Mohammed Hussein Fadlallah: Spiritual leader.

Hasan Izz-Al-Din: One of the hijackers of TWA Flight 847; currently on the FBI's Most Wanted Terrorist list.

Sheikh Abbas Musawi: First operational leader; killed in an Israeli helicopter raid in 1992.

Imad Fayez Mugniyah: Head of security; probably the mastermind of bombings, kidnappings, and hijackings; currently on the FBI's Most Wanted Terrorist list.

Sheikh Seyyed Hassan Nasrallah: Secretary general (the group's operational leader).

dedicated to reclaiming for Palestinian Arabs the land Israel currently possessed, moved into southern Lebanon. It had just been expelled from Jordan because of its militancy and decided to make Lebanon its new headquarters. After the civil war in Lebanon ended, the PLO, led by Yasser Arafat, became bolder in its attacks on Israel, repeatedly launching raids against what it considered to be an occupying power.

It was the radical Palestinians' presence in Lebanon—and Israel's military response to them—that would help give rise to a homegrown terrorist group every bit as dangerous and committed to Israel's destruction as the PLO—Hezbollah.

Resistance
—— Movement or ——
Terrorist Group?

In 1978, Israel was barely thirty years old. In that brief span of time, the tiny country had defended itself against the armies of five nations and utterly destroyed the air forces of Egypt and Syria. In 1967, Israel had soundly defeated Jordan, Syria, and Egypt in a war that lasted only six days and taken from them the Sinai Peninsula, the Golan Heights, the West Bank, and the Gaza Strip. In its short history as a modern nation, Israel had become the greatest military power in the Middle East.

The PLO in Lebanon

Israel could not rest peacefully, however. Southern Lebanon had become home to the PLO, whose primary reason for existence was to destroy Israel and reclaim its land for Arab Palestinians. The Christian government of Lebanon was powerless to stop the PLO, and Syria—the real power behind the Lebanese government— was unwilling to curb it. So, beginning in 1978, the Israeli Defense Force (IDF) felt it had no choice but to march across the border with guns drawn in limited retaliatory attacks.

Even with the help of the South Lebanese Army (SLA)—a Lebanese Christian militia trained and funded by Israel—the IDF could not stamp out the PLO, although the combined forces penetrated far into Lebanese territory. Through the SLA, Israel maintained control of a six- to twelve-mile strip of Southern Lebanon.

The terrorists moved north and continued their strikes. Israel could not be safe as long as the PLO remained a force in Lebanon. Israel decided it needed to focus greater military might on the terrorist group. As a result, on June 6, 1982, Israel launched a large-scale invasion of Lebanon.

Israeli Occupation of Lebanon

The Israeli army marched easily through southern Lebanon, northward to the capital, Beirut. On August 14, 1982, after two months of shelling from land, sea, and air, Israel's troops entered West Beirut. One week later, the PLO began to leave the city. By September 1, nearly all PLO forces were out of Lebanon, dispersed among eight different Arab countries.

Israel was still not convinced, however, that Lebanon could keep similar terrorist groups from attacking its territory. So, even though the UN brought multinational peacekeepers to the country in 1978, Israel kept a defense force in Lebanon to serve as a buffer between Israelis and Palestinian terrorists. Israel declared a large section of the southern portion of the country a security zone and stationed the IDF there. The plan was to bring the fight to the guerrillas in Lebanon before the guerrillas had a chance to slip through the border and attack Israeli villages. Although its troops confined themselves largely to the security zone, Israel was nevertheless occupying a considerable portion of Lebanon's territory. Its forces would remain in the country until May 2000, a total of twenty-two years.

Israel's occupation of Lebanon solved, for the moment at least, the problem of the PLO, but it created another one every bit as dangerous. That threat came not from the Palestinians, but from Shiite Muslims who lived around the Israeli-occupied security zone.

The border between Israel and Lebanon, seen from near the Israeli border town of Metula. This area is the site of frequent cross-border clashes between Lebanese terrorists and the Israeli army. The photograph was taken on March 1, 1999, one day after a Hezbollah attack in southern Lebanon killed four Israeli soldiers. After residents of northern Israel spent the night in bomb shelters for fear of a Hezbollah rocket attack, Israel retaliated by bombing Hezbollah bases deep within Lebanon, including an ammunitions depot north of Israel's self-declared security zone.

Shiite Resistance

Shiite Muslims formed a small minority in Lebanon. In fact, Shiites represent a minority even within the Islamic faith. Shia is a sect of Islam that holds some views that are distinctly different from those of the majority—the Sunni Muslims. Because they were in the minority, Shiites had no political power in Lebanon. The government was primarily Maronite, with some Sunni representation. During the 1975–1976 civil war, however, the Shiites in the south took advantage of the prevailing chaos and began to assert themselves. They joined together under the banner of an organization called Amal.

Amal's purpose was to give Shiites, who had been deprived of economic opportunity and political power in Lebanon, a voice in their own affairs. The Shiites were not happy with the country's Christian Lebanese leaders, the other Muslim factions, or the PLO. All these groups had oppressed the Shiites in one way or another. When Israel invaded, the Shiites had hoped the attackers would overthrow their enemies and quickly depart, leaving the newly strengthened Amal to rule southern Lebanon. Instead, Israel became the new power to be reckoned with in the region.

Israeli occupation could sometimes be harsh. Any resistance was brutally crushed by the army. Dozens of young and middle-aged men were arrested and placed in cold, sunless detention camps. Rumors of torture circulated. Amal rebelled against the occupation—which it once sought as a kind of salvation—with a guerrilla campaign of bombings and kidnappings.

Finding a Patron

Some of the more radical and militant Shiites thought Amal was not doing enough. They remembered the 1979 revolution in Iran, in which Shiites had taken over the government and established Islamic rule. The country was now governed according to the Koran, the holy scripture of the Shiites and all other Muslims. Iran's leaders were no longer politicians, businesspeople, royalty, or military men;

An Iranian protester sets fire to a United States flag, while other demonstrators give a clenched fist salute during an anti-American protest in Tehran, the capital city of Iran, on November 5, 1979. One day earlier, a group of about 500 radical Islamic students had stormed the U.S. Embassy in Tehran and taken 66 American diplomats hostage. Some hostages would be released early on, but 52 Americans would remain in captivity for 444 days before regaining their freedom and returning to the United States.

instead, they were conservative fundamentalist religious scholars and teachers. The radical Lebanese Shiites wondered why the same kind of Islamic fundamentalist revolution couldn't be achieved in Lebanon. Creating an Islamic state was a far better goal, they decided, than simply freeing their land from Israeli domination. A few of these extremists broke away from Amal and formed their own group. They gave it a name that combined political ambition with religious fervor—Hezbollah (in English, the "Party of God").

Like Amal, Hezbollah was small and poorly armed compared with the expertly trained and well-supplied Israeli Defense Force. Iran, interested in both exporting its brand of Islamic revolution to other Arab countries and gaining greater influence in the region, intervened on behalf of the Shiites in Lebanon. In 1982, it sent some of its elite Revolutionary Guard to Lebanon to help the militants in their struggle against the Israelis. Iran also set up training camps for Hezbollah warriors in the Bekaa Valley of Lebanon and in the southern suburbs of Beirut, and supplied the radical organization with money and weapons.

By 1985, Hezbollah had become far more than a band of discontented villagers. It had an organizational structure, clear goals, a specific strategy, and the financial resources to carry out its plans.

Goals and Strategies

Hezbollah's two main objectives were the annihilation of Israel and the creation of an Islamic government in Lebanon. The two separate objectives required two different strategies.

The strategy Hezbollah adopted to achieve Islamic rule in Lebanon was greater involvement in the country's national politics. The group called itself the "Party of God" because it wanted to be seen as a legitimate political party. Its leaders succeeded in 1992 in getting elected to public office, where they could influence and transform the government from within, as a working part of the political system.

To gain popular support, Hezbollah went into poor neighborhoods and gave people what the government had not. It provided

Armed police officers search voters at a polling station in the Shiite Muslim–dominated southern Beirut suburb of Bourj el-Barajneh, on May 24, 1998. In these municipal elections, the first in thirty-five years, the two main political parties of the Shiites—Amal and Hezbollah—fielded rival candidates. Seventy municipalities did not participate in the elections because of Israeli occupation or the displacement of village populations due to wars. The government and the Muslim, pro-Syria Amal movement fared poorly in Mount Lebanon, while Hezbollah and Christians made notable gains.

social services for widows and the disabled, building hospitals and clinics that offered medical care at a very low cost. It operated schools for children who had no other way to obtain an education. It built and staffed orphanages for the many children who had been left without parents during Lebanon's violent civil war. All these

Portrait of a Terrorist: Imad Fayez Mugniyah

- Born July 12, 1962, in Tir Dibba, Lebanon. Father: Sheik Muhammad Jawad Mugniyah, called one of Shia Lebanon's best jurists (judges).
- Dropped out of high school.
- Joined Yasser Arafat's Fatah and later Force 17, Arafat's personal security service.
- When the PLO was expelled from Lebanon in 1982, joined Hezbollah, reporting to Ali Akbar Mohtashemi-Pour, Iran's ambassador to Syria.
- Learned bomb making from brother-in-law, Mustapha Badr-el-Din.
- Two of his brothers killed by car bombs for which he blamed the United States and Israel.
- Masterminded U.S. Embassy and Marine barracks suicide bombings in 1983 and many other attacks.
- Led 1980s kidnappings under alias "Hajj."
- Masterminded and participated in TWA Flight 847 hijacking in 1985.
- Masterminded and may have participated in hijacking of Kuwait Airlines Flight 221 bound for Bangkok from Kuwait and carrying three members of the Kuwaiti royal family. While taking the plane to Iran, Cyprus, and finally Algiers, the hijackers demanded the release of Mugniyah's brother-in-law and sixteen other Shiite prisoners held in Kuwait. In Cyprus, two passengers were killed and their bodies dumped on the runway. The Algerian and Iranian governments and the PLO arranged for safe passage for the hijackers, and the remaining passengers and crew were released.

services were of relatively high quality, were operated professionally, and were made available to everyone—Muslim and Christian alike. Hezbollah quickly became respected as a force for positive social change among many Lebanese citizens.

Encouraging the adoption of Islamic rule was only one of Hezbollah's goals, however. The complete obliteration of Israel was another. Hezbollah would begin working toward this objective by first forcing Israeli soldiers out of Lebanon. They would also try to expel the U.S. and French soldiers who were stationed there as UN peacekeepers. This was a mission that eventually earned Hezbollah the support of many in their country. The removal of foreigners from Lebanese soil was considered a just cause. The fight against occupation allowed Hezbollah to paint itself as a resistance movement. Its leaders claimed to represent ordinary citizens resisting Israeli oppression.

Hezbollah's membership does indeed consist of ordinary citizens. Only one-third of the 1,500 members work in the organization full-time. The rest live in stable homes, have loving families, work at regular jobs, and enjoy normal social lives. When the call goes out that Hezbollah needs them, however, they answer immediately, leaving their safe, normal lives behind, perhaps forever.

Hezbollah vs.
the United States

In 1982, when Hezbollah was born, its leaders could easily identify their friends and their enemies. Syria was their friend, because Syria controlled Lebanon and allowed—even encouraged—their operations against Israel. Iran was their sponsor, supplying money, weapons, training, and inspiration. Their greatest enemy, of course, was Israel. The Christian Lebanese government and its militias were also considered to be enemies because they tended to side with Israel against Palestinian and other Arab groups. And the peacekeepers were enemies—the mostly U.S. and French troops from the hated West that permitted Israel to remain in their country.

Sending in Peacekeepers

The peacekeepers had come at the request of the Lebanese government. When the PLO was being evacuated from Beirut, the government wanted to ensure that no violence would erupt between the departing Palestinians and the victorious Israelis. So Lebanon asked the United Nations to send a multinational army to act as a buffer between the two combatants and enforce a tense peace. French, U.S., and Italian forces came and stayed for only two weeks. Once the PLO had been fully evacuated, the multinational force left soon after, not wanting to get further embroiled in the troubled country's politics.

Just four days later, however, another crisis brought the peace-keepers back. On September 14, 1982, the president-elect of Lebanon, Bashir al-Jumayyil, was assassinated. Assuming Palestinians were to blame, a Christian Lebanese militia raided the Sabra and Shatila refugee camps of west Beirut and killed hundreds of innocent civilians. Israel, whose troops occupied west Beirut, did nothing to stop the carnage. Faced with a newly lead-erless government and violence in the streets, Lebanon again asked for the help of other countries. The United States and France volunteered their services once more.

Hezbollah viewed the foreign armies not as peacekeepers who would put a halt to the indiscriminate murder of Arabs but as agents of Western imperialism. The presence of French and U.S. troops was seen as evidence of Western governments' desire to take over Lebanon. In addition, foreign troops were seen as being both friendly with Israel and a serious threat to the establishment of Islamic rule. The UN peacekeepers quickly became the scapegoat upon which Hezbollah could load all its grievances. As a result, Hezbollah focused much of its efforts on ridding Lebanon of the U.S. and French troops.

U.S. Embassy Bombing

The first major Hezbollah attack against U.S. interests in Lebanon was made on April 18, 1983. The target was the U.S. Embassy, a seven-story building in Beirut. The weapon was a van that had been stolen from the embassy almost a year earlier, loaded with 2,000 pounds of explosives. A Hezbollah commando drove to the embassy at about 1:00 PM, when many people inside were having lunch. He rammed the van into the building, and the impact set off the charges.

The collapsed remains of the United States Embassy in West Beirut, Lebanon, following a Hezbollah suicide truck bombing on April 18, 1983. Among the seventeen Americans killed were one U.S. Marine embassy guard, a journalist, several State Department employees, the entire Middle East contingent of the U.S. Central Intelligence Agency (CIA), including the CIA's Middle East director, and several U.S. Army trainers. Most of the victims were at lunch and were killed when the building collapsed.

When the explosives were detonated, the front of the embassy was ripped apart. Sixty-three people were killed, most when the upper floors of the building collapsed on them. Only seventeen of the victims were Americans; the rest were Lebanese.

Encouraged by this success, Hezbollah leaders looked for other Western targets in Lebanon to attack. They settled on two buildings that housed peacekeepers: One contained U.S. Marines, the other held French paratroopers.

Marine Barracks Bombing

The Aviation Safety Building was a four-story cement and steel structure set on a lot at the Beirut airport. At different times in its history, it had housed Syrian troops, Palestinian guerrillas, and the Israeli army. In October 1983, it was the headquarters for the 1,600 U.S. Marines stationed in Lebanon.

On Sunday morning, October 23, just after 6:00 AM, most of those marines, assuming their headquarters were completely safe and well defended, were sleeping in the barracks. Telescopes mounted on the roof enabled lookouts to spot any trouble from a distance. No unauthorized person should have been able to get close to the barracks because a large lot separated the marines from the heavy traffic of the airport terminal. A barbed wire fence cut across the lot, keeping out any intruders. Beyond the barbed wire was a bunker surrounded by sandbags and protected by Lebanese soldiers and a marine. Anyone who got past these guards was stopped by a wrought iron fence—a six-foot-high barrier that surrounded the building. Beyond that was another wall of sandbags behind which marines could crouch and fire. Fifteen feet farther, at the door of

United States Marines carry a victim of the October 23, 1983, Hezbollah bombing of the marine headquarters in Beirut, Lebanon. A truck loaded with more than 2,000 pounds of explosives was driven into the compound by a Hezbollah suicide bomber, destroying the compound, killing 241 U.S. military personnel, and seriously wounding 80 others. Twenty-one of the American victims were returned to the United States and buried near one another in Arlington National Cemetery. A Cedar of Lebanon tree is planted near their gravesites, commemorating their sacrifice.

the barracks, a guard stood in a wood and glass sentry box that was reinforced with more sandbags. Even with the suicide bombing at the U.S. Embassy six months earlier, the marines still felt safe behind all these layers of security.

At 6:20 that Sunday morning, however, their illusion of safety was shattered. About a half mile from the barracks, a Mercedes pickup truck driven by a Hezbollah guerrilla approached a Lebanese army checkpoint outside the airport. If the soldier on duty had examined the truck, he might have discovered the more than 2,000 pounds of TNT inside, made ten times more potent by the addition of compressed gas. Trucks were a common sight around the airport, however, and the soldier waved the pickup through without a search.

Just a few yards from the airport, the truck turned off into an unguarded parking lot in front of the Aviation Safety Building. Once in the parking lot, the pickup circled twice, revved its engine, accelerated, and drove straight for the barracks. The Hezbollah terrorist drove right over the barbed wire, around the sandbagged bunker, through the locked gate of the iron fence, and around the second sandbag barricade. The guard posted at the barracks door fired his M-15 rifle at least five times at the truck. But the young driver simply smiled and kept going. He crashed through the door of the barracks and into the lobby. There he detonated his load, bringing all four stories to the ground and killing 241 marines.

French Paratroop Barracks Bombing

The blast woke people all over Beirut. Two miles north of the Aviation Safety Building, in the suburb of Jnah, the explosion startled soldiers of the Third Company of the Sixth French Parachute Infantry Regiment. They ran to the windows of their barracks. While they gazed south toward the airport, less than two minutes after the attack on the marines, another suicide truck bomb demolished the French quarters.

A French paratrooper holds the hand of one of his comrades who is still trapped in debris following the Hezbollah car bombing of the French paratroopers' barracks on October 23, 1983, in Beirut, Lebanon. Coming just minutes after the bombing of the U.S. Marine headquarters nearby, this nearly simultaneous attack killed fifty-eight French troops.

The barracks building was huge—eight stories high with cement walls three feet thick—but the six-hundred-pound bomb was strong. It lifted the barracks off its foundation and hurled it twenty feet. It crushed all eight floors and shattered the windows of buildings that stood several blocks away. This second truck bomb killed fifty-eight people.

Hezbollah: Some Radical Islamic Perspectives

"The Iranian leadership considers Hezbollah as an extension of itself in the Middle East."

—Ghassan Ben-Jeddou, Tehran correspondent, Qatari Al-Jazira television station, from Lebanon's *Daily Star*, November 15, 2001

"Martyrdom is the weapon that God gave to this nation . . . In the Israeli society, there are no civilians. They are all invaders, occupiers, land violators and partners in crimes and massacres. Therefore, we should pursue this road without any hesitation."

—Seyyed Hassan Nasrallah, spiritual guide of Hezbollah, as reported by United Press International, December 14, 2001

"This [1983 Marine barracks bombing] attack . . . was not in a strict sense a terrorist operation. It was a military operation, producing no civilian casualties."

—Spokesman for Muslim Public Affairs Council as quoted in Steven Emerson's *American Jihad: The Terrorists Living Among Us*

From an Interview between *CBS News'* Dan Rather and Hezbollah Deputy Secretary General Naim Qassem:

Rather: What is Hezbollah? Is it in any way a terrorist organization?

Qassem: We have never been a terrorist organization. We consider ourselves a resistance movement against occupation. Israel is the terrorist because they are killing children, women, and old people. And the United States, too, is a terrorist insofar as it supports Israel.

—CBS Evening News, April 17, 2002

Aftermath

The U.S. response to the attack on its soldiers and property was immediate retaliation and defiance. The battleship USS *New Jersey* rained down mortar shells on Beirut for a short time, and President Ronald Reagan declared that the marines would remain in Lebanon as part of the multinational peacekeeping force. The Lebanese government, however, weary of the internal strife tearing apart the nation, asked the United States to leave. By February 26, 1984, just four months after the devastating attack, all U.S. Marines had left Lebanon.

With their departure, Hezbollah scored a major triumph. It had pioneered a new weapon—suicide bombing—that was brutally successful. It had chased off what it considered to be an imperialist invader and delivered a stinging blow to a great Western power. It had killed more Americans than any other terrorist group up to that point—a sinister record that stood until September 11, 2001. Hezbollah had its first taste of victory, and it was hungry for more.

Evolution of a Terrorist Organization

W hen Hezbollah drove the United States from Lebanon, it was still a small group with more daring than resources. From its founding, however, Iran had been helping to build and shape it into a far more dangerous and deadly organization. With funding and training from Iran, Hezbollah slowly transformed itself from a guerrilla band of impoverished villagers into a highly efficient, well-supplied, and widely feared link in a network of international terrorism.

A Larger Mission and New Tactics

In its early years, Hezbollah was concerned almost entirely with local issues—namely with the military presence of Israel and Western countries in Lebanon. The suicide bombings of the U.S. Embassy, the U.S. Marine barracks, and the French paratroop barracks were all designed to both protest and bring an end to foreign occupation of Lebanese territory. As Iran's influence grew stronger, however, Hezbollah's vision broadened. Throughout the mid- and late 1980s, Hezbollah undertook missions in Lebanon that would support Iranian interests.

At the time, Iran was fighting a prolonged war with its neighbor Iraq. Iran wanted money and weapons, which would allow it to continue to fight the long and costly war, and the release of some of its fighters who were jailed in several different countries.

CHAPTER 4

Lebanon had something Iran could use as a bargaining chip: vulnerable Western citizens.

Kidnappings

To help its sponsor Iran—and at the same time continue to frighten and humiliate the West—Hezbollah began a kidnapping spree in February 1984. Over the next four years, Hezbollah captured a total of at least thirty foreigners, including seventeen Americans. They came from all walks of life: professors at the American University of Beirut, a diplomat, a journalist, a hospital director, a priest, and a Presbyterian missionary. All that mattered was that they were Westerners.

After being kidnapped, the Western hostages were blindfolded, chained at their wrists and ankles, and thrown into the closets and basements of various buildings in the slums of Shiite dominated south Beirut. Sometimes they were chained to radiators. Some had cots to sleep on, others had to make do with mats on the floor. Most were kept in makeshift cells all by themselves for many long months. In some cases, several hostages were held in the same building. The cells were next to each other, and the prisoners could hear each other coughing from the cold and dankness or ranting deliriously. At times, they were allowed to sit together, but they usually had to keep their blindfolds on. The hostages were beaten mercilessly, usually for no apparent reason. They survived on old bread, cheese, and tea.

Most hostages survived and were eventually released, but three Americans died in their Beirut prisons. Three of the kidnapped Westerners managed to escape. The rest were eventually freed, but

Security officers cover the remains of three bodies found buried in the garden of a house outside Ankara, Turkey, on January 20, 2000, after Hezbollah militants confessed to hiding corpses there. In addition to the use of kidnapping to have political demands met, Hezbollah operatives in Turkey (who hope to establish an independent Islamic Kurdish state in the southeastern part of the country) also use kidnapping, torture, and even murder of fellow Muslims to enforce a strict interpretation of Islam. By February 1, 2000, the bodies of forty-nine people, tortured and executed by fundamentalists, had been found throughout Turkey.

only after years of psychological and physical torture. Terry Anderson, chief Middle East correspondent for the Associated Press, was held the longest. Captured in March 1985, he was the last to be released, in December 1991, after 2,454 days in captivity.

Several of the kidnappings worked as planned and served Iran well. After two French hostages were freed in 1985, France repaid an old debt to Iran of $330 million. Three Americans were released in exchange for a secret U.S. arms deal that provided Iran with a fresh supply of weapons with which to wage war against Iraq, which was then considered a moderate Arab country. This deal was especially startling since Iran had been the United States's enemy ever since the hostage crisis of 1979–1980, in which Iranian Islamic militants seized the U.S. Embassy in Tehran and held fifty-two Americans hostage for 444 days.

Hezbollah proved as successful at kidnapping as it was at suicide bombing. Kidnapping individuals and holding them for long periods of time was physically draining, however, and its rewards could take years to materialize. Hezbollah became interested in devising a quicker way to achieve the same ends. How could several hostages be taken at once and the group's demands be met immediately? Hezbollah found its solution on TWA Flight 847.

Hijacking

On June 14, 1985, TWA Flight 847 left Athens, Greece, at 10:00 AM with 143 passengers. It was to be a short trip to Rome, Italy.

Minutes after the "fasten seat belts" sign flashed off, however, two men sprang from their seats, cursing and threatening Americans, and dashed to the front of the airplane. When they reached the senior flight attendant, they slammed her against the cockpit door. All she could see were a gun and a hand grenade. One of the hijackers jumped up and kicked her chest with both feet while the other grabbed her head and pounded it against the door.

One of the three Hezbollah hijackers aboard TWA Flight 847 points his pistol toward a crew from ABC News as they approach the jet for an interview at Beirut International Airport, Lebanon, on June 19, 1985. The hijacking ordeal would last almost three weeks for thirty-nine of the plane's passengers, who would be removed from the plane and held captive for seventeen days in Shiite hideouts in Beirut before finally being released. *Inset*: Two Hezbollah hijackers, who escaped after the hijacking ended, are still on the FBI's Most Wanted Terrorists list.

Mugniyah

Izz-al-Din

Most Wanted Terrorists sought for the hijacking of TWA Flight 847 on June 14, 1985

To keep them from shooting the lock off, the terrified flight attendant opened the cockpit door.

After threatening the pilots, the hijackers paced wildly up and down the aisles, beating crew and passengers alike, women and children as well as men. They struck them with their fists, hit them with grenades, and whipped them with pistols. One elderly woman was karate-kicked in the face. The terrorists repeatedly shouted one of the few English phrases they knew: "We have come to die."

To keep the passengers from conspiring against them, the hijackers kept moving them around, forcing strong men to sit by the windows with women, children, and the elderly next to them, blocking their way to the aisles. No one was permitted to speak. For hours at a time, they were forced to crouch down so that their heads were below the backs of their seats, making communication and joint action among the passengers difficult.

For two days the plane shuttled back and forth between airports in Algeria and Beirut as the 747 took on additional fuel and more hijackers and freed several hostages. At each stop, the hijackers called for the release from Israeli jails of 766 Lebanese Shiites and the withdrawal of Israeli forces from Lebanon. Israel had intended to free the prisoners when the situation in Lebanon calmed, but did not want to give in to the demands of terrorists. Neither did the United States. So the frustrated hijackers continued to hold the airplane and terrorize its passengers and crew.

In an attempt to direct the greatest terror against Jews and Americans, they collected the passports and identification papers of all the passengers. They isolated seven they thought were Jewish and seven who were American military personnel. Vowing loudly that "one American must die," they bound the arms and

United States President Ronald Reagan and his wife Nancy greeting the former hostages of TWA Flight 847 as they debark from the plane that flew them home, at Andrews Air Force Base in July 1985. Reagan, who had referred to the hijackers as "thugs, murderers, and barbarians," also warned other terrorists against any similar action. In a televised address, he said, "Terrorists, be on notice: we will fight back against you in Lebanon and elsewhere."

wrists of U.S. Navy diver Robert Stethem. During a stop in Algeria, one of the hijackers beat Stethem while another waved a grenade for all the passengers to see. Hours later, on a stop in Beirut, the terrorists yanked the navy diver out of his seat. They shot him twice and rolled his body out the door to the tarmac below. Breaking the tense silence, one began chanting a song of victory. Six passengers with "Jewish sounding" names or military identification papers were taken off the aircraft and held captive by members of the terrorist group Islamic Jihad. They would later be rescued by a U.S. military antiterrorist group, Delta Force.

In the end, Hezbollah was again victorious. Some of the hostages were released at various stops, but thirty-nine were held until the hijacking ended three days after it began and then removed from the plane, separated into smaller groups, and held in several locations for another seventeen days in a Shiite neighborhood of Beirut. After Israel released thirty-one shiite prisoners, the thirty-nine hostages were released.

Expelling Israel

Despite its growing list of successful strikes, Hezbollah had still not achieved its primary aims: expelling Israel from Lebanon and establishing an Islamic state. So in the 1990s, Hezbollah directed most of its energies toward these goals. In 1992, the Party of God entered politics and won eight seats in Lebanon's parliament. By 2002, the party had twelve seats in the governing body.

While its politicians were winning elections, its fighters were terrorizing Israeli soldiers in the south. They were making remote-controlled bombs disguised as rocks, planting land mines near Israeli positions, and shooting into Israeli guard posts. They were firing Katyusha rockets (Soviet-made devices with a range of up to thirty-eight miles) into Israel. Each time Hezbollah struck, Israel retaliated. But Hezbollah was launching attacks more and more often, and Israel was losing more and more soldiers.

Many Israelis began to conclude that there was nothing to be gained by remaining in Lebanon. Their leaders agreed and tried to arrange a peace treaty with Lebanon and Syria, which had 25,000 soldiers in Lebanon. Peace talks soon disintegrated, however. So Israel called on the United Nations to determine exactly where the border between Lebanon and Israel actually was. The UN drew a "blue line" on a map of the region beyond which Israel agreed to pull back. Hezbollah was not happy with the line, but it was ecstatic that Israel promised to leave.

On May 23 and May 24, 2000, Israel withdrew its troops from the security zone it had created in southern Lebanon. Immediately, thousands of dancing and cheering Lebanese rushed in to reclaim the area. Many waved the yellow banner of Hezbollah. The group had done what no Arab country had ever come close to doing: It had defeated Israel militarily. Its relentless guerrilla warfare had driven its enemy out of the country. This gave Hezbollah hero status among many other Middle Eastern terrorist groups, Arab governments, and Muslims throughout the region.

Connecting with Others

Because of its victories and the resulting media attention, Hezbollah's membership grew, as did its prestige among many Muslims. Other radical groups looked to it for help in developing and carrying out their own terrorist attacks. Since Hezbollah was committed to the destruction of Israel and the establishment of Islamic states, it gladly cooperated with a number of like-minded groups outside Lebanon. In conjunction with other terrorist organizations, Hezbollah bombed the Israeli Embassy in Buenos Aires, Argentina, in 1992, killing twenty-nine people. It blew up a Jewish community center in the same city in 1994, killing eighty-six

Young Lebanese members of the Hezbollah movement participate in a military parade on the occasion of Jerusalem Day in the southern suburbs of Beirut on December 22, 2000. The event, which is held on the last Friday of the Muslim holy month of Ramadan, commemorates the capture of Arab East Jerusalem by Israel in 1967 and is observed with protest rallies and parades in most Middle East countries.

Israel and Hezbollah Timeline

May 15, 1948   Israel becomes a nation. More than 700,000 Palestinian refugees flee Israel.

1975–1976   Civil war in Lebanon.

1978   Israel enters Lebanon and occupies areas adjacent to its border with Lebanon.

June 6, 1982   Israel invades Lebanon and occupies portions of southern Lebanon for the next eighteen years.

April 18, 1983   Hezbollah bombs U.S. Embassy in West Beirut, killing 63.

October 23, 1983   Hezbollah bombs U.S. Marine barracks in Beirut, killing 241, and French paratroop barracks, killing 58.

September 20, 1984   Hezbollah bombs U.S. Embassy annex in East Beirut, killing 24.

1984–1988   Seventeen Americans and several other Westerners are kidnapped.

February 16, 1985   Hezbollah states its platform in an open letter to the "Downtrodden of Lebanon and the World."

June 14, 1985   TWA Flight 847 hijacked, U.S. Navy diver killed.

March 17, 1992   Israeli Embassy in Buenos Aires, Argentina, bombed; 29 killed.

September 1992   Hezbollah wins eight seats in Lebanon's parliament.

July 18, 1994   Jewish community center in Buenos Aires, Argentina, bombed; 86 killed.

June 25, 1996   Khobar Towers in Riyadh, Saudi Arabia, bombed; 19 U.S. airmen killed.

May 23–24, 2000   Israel withdraws from Lebanon.

people. It also built the bomb that blasted the Khobar Towers in Saudi Arabia, an apartment building that housed U.S. troops in June 1996, killing nineteen and wounding hundreds more.

In the 1990s, Hezbollah was training members of the terrorist groups Al Qaeda, Hamas, and the Palestinian Islamic Jihad in the use of explosives. Iran still provided the financing, but Hezbollah did the actual work. Its leaders were meeting with Osama bin Laden as early as 1993 to plan joint activities. Hezbollah was willing to work with any group committed to violent acts against Israel. It supported the PLO, even though the organization was secular (having no religious orientation) and made up mainly of Sunni Muslims, because in its early days the PLO was dedicated to the annihilation of Israel. (During peace negotiations in the mid-1990s, however, the PLO officially condemned terror attacks against Israel and acknowledged the country's right to exist.)

Hezbollah has come a long way as a terrorist organization. It is no longer a small gang of villagers hurling crude, homemade rockets against Israeli soldiers. Hezbollah has become a highly organized, well-financed, and extremely disciplined link in the network of global terrorism. Over time, the group has only become more efficient, effective, and experienced. Its continued growth and development sounds an ominous note for the prospects of peace in the Middle East and security for Westerners everywhere.

Conclusion

After the September 11, 2001, terrorist attacks on the United States, the Federal Bureau of Investigation (FBI) published a list of twenty-two of America's most wanted terrorists. Three of them belonged to Hezbollah. In October of the same year, Secretary of State Colin L. Powell released a list of twenty-five groups designated as foreign terrorist organizations—groups that have undertaken murderous attacks against innocent civilians, many of which have an international reach and are funded by foreign governments. Hezbollah was one of them. How far do the tentacles of this Lebanese group reach?

Hezbollah cells (small clusters of terrorist operatives) have been found in Europe, the Far East, and North and South America. In the United States, Hezbollah is thought to have active members in Detroit, Michigan; Philadelphia, Pennsylvania; Charlotte, North Carolina; Potomac, Maryland; Washington, D.C.; and New York City. For the most part, these cells do not conduct terrorist activities, but they recruit fighters and raise funds for Hezbollah operations in the Middle East. Some of the money is gathered from the donations of Lebanese people living in these U.S. cities, but most comes from criminal activity, such as illegal cigarette smuggling and sales.

Hezbollah's fund-raising activities in the United States are one reason that President George W. Bush and the State Department placed the group on its list of foreign terrorist organizations. Anyone living in the United States who provides support of any

U.S. Marshals escort Mohamad Youssef Hammoud *(top center)* into the federal courthouse in Charlotte, North Carolina, on May 20, 2002. Hammoud was charged under a 1996 antiterrorism law with providing material support to Hezbollah. He was also charged with money laundering, cigarette smuggling, immigration fraud, and other charges. He was convicted on the cigarette smuggling charges in June 2002 and faces up to 155 years in prison.

kind to a group on this list is subject to federal prosecution. Another reason for Hezbollah's appearance on the list is its continued attacks on Israel. At least 10,000 rockets and missiles are hidden in southern Lebanon, aimed at Israel and able to be deployed on a moment's notice. Hezbollah warriors stand in observation posts all along the fence that marks the border with Israel

An Israeli soldier *(foreground)* guards the Israeli-Lebanese border, near Metulla, Israel, while an armed Hezbollah member patrols the Lebanese side, near the village of Kfar Kila, on May 24, 2000. As is a common occurrence along the shared border, dozens of Hezbollah members were gathered at the fence that day, shouting anti-Israeli slogans and hoping to provoke a violent reaction that would discredit the Israeli army. In this instance, Israeli forces declined to take action.

with rifles and anti-aircraft guns at the ready. Almost daily the guns go off, and Israeli towns are showered with shrapnel. A third reason Hezbollah is on the U.S. list of foreign terrorist organizations is its support of the radical Palestinian groups Hamas and Islamic Jihad, which operate in the West Bank and Gaza Strip and often unleash suicide bombers on Israeli cities and towns.

Conclusion

After the list was made public on October 5, 2001, Hezbollah's leader Sheikh Seyyed Hassan Nasrallah called the United States the "Great Satan," according to United Press International, and told his followers: "I say to every member of Hezbollah: Be happy and proud that your party has been placed on the list of terrorist organizations as the U.S. views it."

Hezbollah has continued to fight Israeli troops. According to the United Nations, Israel no longer holds any land in Lebanon, but Hezbollah disputes that claim. As long as Israel has soldiers stationed in the Shebaa Farms area of Lebanon, Hezbollah will continue to call itself a resistance movement, fighting against Israeli occupation of Lebanese land. Even if Israeli forces were to withdraw from that tiny strip of territory (which it considers Syrian territory captured during the 1967 Six-Day War), the group has vowed to continue its campaign against Israel by providing aid to Palestinian groups. Indeed, in early 2001, a Hezbollah-owned ship containing arms bound for the Palestinian territories was intercepted by Israel; it is thought that the weapons were purchased and the delivery arranged by the terrorist group. Hezbollah has pledged to not give up its attacks until Israel is destroyed and Islamic governments rule over the entire Middle East.

And Israel, every bit as defiant as Hezbollah, has proclaimed it will never leave the land it has fought so long and hard to call its own. The United States has vowed to never surrender to terror. Given the stubborn determination of all parties, it seems likely that this new kind of war will rage on—without resolution—for years to come.

Glossary

anti-Semitism   Prejudice against and hatred of Jews.

armistice   A cease-fire agreement by both sides in a conflict; a truce.

cell   A small unit of operatives within a terrorist organization.

guerrilla   A person who fights as a soldier but is not part of any formal army and uses irregular methods such as hijacking, kidnapping, ambush, and suicide bombing.

Holocaust   The deliberate and systematic attempt of the Nazis to kill all Jews during World War II (1939–1945) that resulted in the deaths of six million Jews and other persecuted minorities.

imperialism   The attempt by one government to exert economic or political control over other countries.

Islam   A religion founded in Arabia based on the teachings of Muhammad, considered a prophet of Allah (God).

Israeli Defense Force (IDF)   The army of the state of Israel.

Maronite   A sect of Catholicism based in Lebanon.

militancy   The tendency to promote war and conflict.

militia   A military force that is not part of a country's regular army, usually used in emergencies.

missile   Any weapon that is thrown or projected against a target.

mortar A weapon that fires heavy, explosive shells high into the air and is angled so that the shells drop on the intended target.

Muslim Someone or something that follows the teachings of Islam.

Palestine Liberation Organization (PLO) The political body representing Palestinian Arabs in their attempt to reclaim land from the state of Israel. It was formed in 1964 by several refugee groups and is led by Yasser Arafat.

Palestinian A person originally from the Arabian Peninsula whose ancestors had moved in and around the area now occupied by Israel.

rocket A high-explosive bomb, or guided missile, that travels under its own power after it is launched, until it reaches its target.

Shiite A member of the Shia sect of Islam.

shrapnel Fragments from a mortar or rocket shell.

South Lebanese Army (SLA) The army of southern Lebanon, supplied by and friendly to Israel. The SLA ceased to exist after May 2000, when Israel withdrew from southern Lebanon.

Sunni A follower of the original, orthodox form of Islam.

tarmac The pavement on airport runways.

Zionism The movement to establish Israel as a Jewish state.

For More Information

Central Intelligence Agency (CIA)
Office of Public Affairs
Washington, DC 20505
(703) 482-0623
Web site: http://www.cia.gov

Centre for the Study of Terrorism and Political Violence
Department of International Relations
University of St. Andrews
St. Andrews, Fife KY16 9AL
United Kingdom
Web site: http://www.st-and.ac.uk/academic/intrel/research/cstpv/

Council on American-Islamic Relations (CAIR)
453 New Jersey Avenue SE
Washington, DC 20003
(202) 488-8787
Web site: http://www.cair-net.org

Federal Bureau of Investigation (FBI)
J. Edgar Hoover Building
935 Pennsylvania Avenue NW
Washington, DC 20535-0001

(202) 324-3000
Web site: http://www.fbi.gov

Federation of American Scientists (FAS)
Intelligence Resource Program
1717 K Street NW, Suite 209
Washington, DC 20036
(202) 454-4691
Web site: http://www.fas.org/irp/index.html

International Policy Institute for Counter-Terrorism
The Interdisciplinary Center Herzlia
P.O. Box 167
Herzlia, Israel 46150
Web site: http://www.ict.org.il

National Security Agency (NSA)
Public Affairs Office
9800 Savage Road
Fort George G. Meade, MD 20755-6779
(301) 688-6524
Web site: http://www.nsa.gov

National Security Institute (NSI)
116 Main Street, Suite 200
Medway, MA 02053
(508) 533-9099
Web site: http://nsi.org

Office of the Coordinator for Counterterrorism
Office of Public Affairs, Room 2509
U.S. Department of State
2201 C Street NW
Washington, DC 20520
Web site: http://www.state.gov/s/ct

Terrorist Group Profiles
Dudley Knox Library
Naval Post Graduate School
411 Dyer Road
Monterey, CA 93943
Web site: http://library.nps.navy.mil/home

Web Sites

Due to the changing nature of Internet links, the Rosen Publishing Group, Inc., has developed an online list of Web sites related to the subject of this book. This site is updated regularly. Please use this link to access the list:

http://www.rosenlinks.com/iwmito/lehe/

For Further Reading

Altman, Linda Jacobs. *The Creation of Israel*. San Diego, CA: Lucent Books, 1998.

Anita, Ganeri. *I Remember Palestine*. Minneapolis, MN: Econo-Clad Books, 1999.

Cahill, Mary Jane. *Lebanon*. Broomall, PA: Chelsea House Publishers, 1998.

Greenberg, Keith Elliot. *Terrorism*. Brookfield, CT: Millbrook, 1994.

Jamieson, Alison. *Terrorism*. New York: Thompson Learning, 1995.

Penney, Sue. *Islam*. Crystal Lake, IL: Heinemann Library, 2001.

Ries, Julien. *The World of Islam*. Broomall, PA: Chelsea House Publishers, 2002.

Roden, Katie, Flick Killerby, and Rob Shone. *Terrorism*. Brookfield, CT: Millbrook, 1997.

Sheehan, Sean. *Lebanon*. Tarrytown, NY: Benchmark Books, 1997.

Spencer, William. *Islamic Fundamentalism in the Modern World*. Brookfield, CT: Millbrook Press, 1995.

Wagner, Heather Lehr. *Israel and the Arab World*. Broomall, PA: Chelsea House, 2002.

Wormser, Richard. *American Islam: Growing Up Muslim in America*. New York: Walker, 1994.

Bibliography

Anderson, Terry A. *Den of Lions: Memoirs of Seven Years*. New York: The Crown Publishing Group, 1993.

Ashwood, Thomas M. *Terror in the Skies*. New York: Stein & Day, 1987.

Blanford, Nicholas. "Emboldened by U.S. Jibes, Hizbullah Prepares for War: As US and Israel Hold Talks, Hizbullah Is Amassing Weapons Near Israel's Border." *The Christian Science Monitor*, February 8, 2002.

Dalal, Saoud. "Nasrallah: Suicide Operations 'Only Road.'" United Press International. December 14, 2001. Retrieved May 2002 (http://www.upi.com/print.cfm?StoryID= 14122001-095921-6930r).

Emerson, Steven. *American Jihad: The Terrorists Living Among Us*. New York: The Free Press, 2002.

Friedman, Thomas L. "Beirut Death Toll at 161 Americans; French Casualties Rise in Bombings; Reagan Insists Marines Will Remain; Buildings Blasted." *The New York Times*, October 24, 1983.

Heymann, Philip B. *Terrorism and America: A Commonsense Strategy for a Democratic Society*. Cambridge, MA: MIT Press, 2000.

"Hezbollah Proud to Be on U.S. Terror List." United Press International, November 4, 2001. Retrieved May 2002 (http://www.upi.com/view.cfm?StoryID=04112001-010538-7383r).

Bibliography

"Israel Alleges PA-Iranian Strategic Deal," United Press International, February 10, 2002. Retrieved May 2002 (http://www.upi.com/view.cfm?StoryID=10022002-040121-5543r).

Jaber, Hala. *Hezbollah*. New York: Columbia University Press, 1997.

Moore, Claire. "Remembering Beirut." ABC News.com. October 22, 2000. Retrieved May 2002 (http://abcnews.go.com/sections/world/DailyNews/beirut_memorial001022.html).

Neff, Donald. "With Release of Terry Anderson, U.S. Hostage Ordeal Ended in Lebanon." *Washington Report*, December 1995.

Pillar, Paul R. *Terrorism and U.S. Foreign Policy*. Washington, DC: The Brookings Institution Press, 2001.

Pipes, Daniel. "The Hezbollah in America: An Alarming Network." *National Review*, August 28, 2000.

Ranstorp, Magnus. *Hizb'Allah in Lebanon: The Politics of the Western Hostage Crisis*. New York: Palgrave Macmillan, 1996.

Rather, Dan. "A Hezbollah Leader Speaks Out." CBSNews.com. April 17, 2002. Retrieved May 2002 (http://www.cbsnews.com/stories/2002/04/17/eveningnews/main506497.shtml).

Saad-Ghorayeb, Amal. *Hizbu'llah: Politics and Religion*. London: Pluto Press, 2002.

Index

Index

Israeli Defense Force (IDF), 12, 14, 17, 18, 22
Izz-Al-Din, Hasan, 16

J
Jerusalem, 9, 11
Jordan, 7, 12, 14, 16, 17

K
Kuwait Airlines Flight 221, hijacking of, 24

L
Lebanon
    civil war in, 15, 16, 20, 23, 48
    Hezbollah members in parliament, 44, 48
    Israeli withdrawal from, 7, 45, 48
    Maronite Christians in, 14, 15, 17, 20, 26
    occupation by Israel, 18, 20, 25, 36, 42, 44–45, 48, 53
    PLO in, 16, 17–18, 24
    Shiite Muslims in, 18, 19–22, 37, 44

M
Maronites, 14, 15, 20
Mohtashemi-Pour, Ali Akbar, 24
Mugniyah, Imad Fayez, 16, 24
Musawi, Sheikh Abbas, 16

N
Nasrallah, Sheikh Seyyed Hassan, 16, 34, 53

P
Palestine/Palestinians, 9–14, 15, 17, 18, 26, 27, 30
    refugees from, 12, 15, 16, 48

Palestine Liberation Organization (PLO), 15–16, 17–18, 20, 24, 26, 49
Powell, Colin, 50

R
Reagan, Ronald, 35
refugee camps, 12, 14, 15, 27

S
September 11, 2001, terrorist attacks, 35, 50
Shebaa Farms, 4–7, 53
Shiite Muslims, 18, 19–22, 24, 37, 42, 44
Six-Day War, 7, 17, 53
South Lebanese Army (SLA), 17
Stethem, Robert, 43–44
suicide bombings, 24, 27–33, 35, 36, 39, 52
Sunni Muslims, 20, 49
Syria, 7, 12, 14, 24, 30, 45, 53
    control of Lebanon by, 15, 17, 26

T
TWA Flight 847, hijacking of, 16, 24, 39–44, 48

U
United Nations, 7, 11, 12, 18, 25, 26–27, 45, 53
United States, 24, 25, 26–32, 35, 36, 42, 53
U.S. Embassy bombing, Beirut, 27–30, 31, 36, 48
U.S. Marine barracks bombing, 30–32, 35, 36, 48

W
West Bank, 11, 12, 17, 52

Z
Zionism, 9, 10, 11

About the Author

Ann Byers is a teacher, writer, and editor. She, her husband, and their four grown children live in California.

Photo Credits

Cover © Hossam Abu Allan/Corbis; p. 1 © Ali Mohamed/AP/Wide World Photos; p. 5 © Roger Wood/Corbis; p. 6 © Haidar Hawila/Corbis; pp. 13, 28–29, 31 © Francoise de Mulder/Corbis; p. 19 © Ruth Fremson/AP/Wide World Photos; p. 21 © Mohammad Sayad/AP/Wide World Photos; p. 23 © Ahmed Azakir/AP/Wide World Photos; pp. 33, 41 (inset), 52 © Corbis; p. 38 © Ecvet Atik/AP/Wide World Photos; pp. 40–41 © Herve Merliac/AP/Wide World Photos; p. 43 © TimePix; pp. 46–47 © Ramzi Haidar/Corbis; p. 51 © Chuck Burton/AP/Wide World Photos.

Series Design and Layout

Nelson Sá